CITY
Through the Ages

PHILIP STEELE

Illustrated by
**IVAN LAPPER, ANDREW HOWAT and
GORDON DAVIDSON**

Troll Associates

Library of Congress Cataloging-in-Publication Data

Steele, Philip
   City through the ages / by Philip Steele, illustrated by Ivan
Lapper, Andrew Howat, and Gordon Davidson
    p.   cm
   Summary: Traces the development of a fictitious city in Western
Europe from the Stone Age through the present and future.
   ISBN 0-8167-2727-9 (lib. bdg.)   ISBN 0-8167-2728-7 (pbk.)
   1. Cities and towns–History–Juvenile literature. [1. Cities
and towns. 2. Civilization–History.] I. Lapper, Ivan, ill.
II. Howat, Andrew, ill. III. Davidson, Gordon, ill. IV. Title.
HT111.S714 1993
307.76–dc20   91-37350

Published by Troll Associates
© 1994 Eagle Books

Design by James Marks

Printed in the U.S.A.

10 9 8 7 6 5 4 3 2 1

Introduction

This is the story of a city and of the people who built it. You will not find the city on any map, but there are many like it in the world today. Between modern buildings of glass and steel you may discover narrow streets built in the 1800s, or ruined town walls dating back to the Middle Ages.

This story is set in western Europe, but at different periods cities also grew up in other parts of the world, from Mexico to India and China. Many Europeans later settled in the Americas and in Australia and founded new towns and cities there, far from their former homes.

Contents

Cave dwellers

Landscapes change over millions of years. At one time this land was covered in swamps and jungles. Strange animals lived and died here, long before humans were seen. In 48,000 B.C. the land was covered by snow and ice. Dense forests of pine stretched from the sea to the rocky slopes of the hills.

One day the peace of the forest was broken by blood-curdling yells, grunts, and whistles. A band of hunters was scrambling over the rocks, their bodies smeared with red ocher. They had killed a long-horned mountain goat.

The hunters were stockier than modern people. They had sloping foreheads and heavy brows. They dragged the broken body of the goat to a great cave in the hills. For thousands of years hunters sheltered in these caves, until the stones were blackened by their fires.

Today we call these hunters Neanderthal people. Caves like these might have been home to 40 or more men, women, and children. On long hunting trips they erected tents or shelters in the open. They wore skins and furs and buried their dead in graves.

Neanderthal people made tools of flint and other hard stones. They chipped and flaked them into shape with stones and antlers, and then sharpened them. They also made spearheads, knives, saws, and scrapers.

A new tribe arrives

What became of the Neanderthal people? Nobody knows. In about 30,000 B.C. a new tribe of people set up their totem, a bear skull, high on the windy ridge. There were great battles and the Neanderthalers were driven deep into the forest. The newcomers looked weaker than the Neanderthalers, but they were swifter, nimbler, and more cunning. They were people like us. They painted on the walls of the caves and made better tools.

By 7500 B.C. the climate had changed again. Hazel trees grew in the woods, which teemed with small game. Fishermen built wooden huts on the banks of the river and thatched them with reed. They made canoes from tree trunks hollowed by axes and fire. Well-beaten tracks ran along the river and through the woods to the ridge.

Sometimes the hunters caught a wild ox, and the feasting lasted for days. In the winter, game was scarce and the villagers often went hungry.

The river bank dwellers of 7500 B.C. caught fish with bone hooks and spears made of antler horn. The river also provided them with ducks and wild geese in season.

Hares, deer, and boar were hunted in the woods and hills. The hunters made weapons of bone and flint, and of wood inset with small stones.

7

A center of trade

Axes felled clearings in the woods. If you stood up on the ridge, columns of smoke could now be seen rising from a number of small villages. The biggest settlement of all could be seen in the distance, guarding the mouth of the river. It was made up of about 30 huts thatched with reeds. In the year 1500 B.C. it was protected by a wooden stockade. Stout poles with sharpened ends defended the settlement from attack.

People still hunted for meat and gathered berries, but farming had now been established in the region for thousands of years. Barley was grown and sheep provided wool and meat. Some tools and weapons were still made of wood and stone, but most were now made of bronze, a mixture of copper and tin. The secret of working these metals was learned from traders from Mediterranean lands.

The town at the mouth of the river grew steadily as a result of trade. Merchants arrived from distant lands. They brought jewelry and pottery. One day they sold the chief a knife made of a hard, gray metal called iron.

8

The Celts

Many peoples had come and gone. All had left their mark on the landscape. There were ancient burial mounds and ditches, feared by many as the haunt of ghosts. These were already ancient when in 450 B.C. a tribe of head-hunting Celts invaded the region in their chariots. Villagers captured in the battles were enslaved.

The Celts were master ironworkers. Iron sickles harvested the barley and heavy wooden plows tilled the soil. By the year 200 B.C., several new villages had appeared on the edge of the forest. These were made up of large round huts thatched with straw.

The Celts built no large towns, but in times of war they would take refuge behind the earth and stockade defenses of their large fort, high on the ridge.

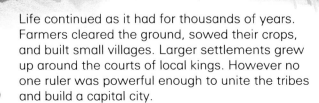

Life continued as it had for thousands of years. Farmers cleared the ground, sowed their crops, and built small villages. Larger settlements grew up around the courts of local kings. However no one ruler was powerful enough to unite the tribes and build a capital city.

Roman town

A new power had grown up, far to the south. In 50 a Roman legion attacked by sea. Celtic charioteers galloped out to meet them, but were hacked to pieces. The line of soldiers moved forward with relentless discipline. The farmsteads of the Celts were soon burned, and the royal fort was stormed. Already the Roman legionaries were digging long ditches and raising the walls of a fort.

By 250 the forest had been cleared. A great town had grown up around the headquarters of the legion. It was the capital of the province. Long, straight roads ran inland.

In the marketplace, or forum, soldiers from Africa and the Middle East mingled with Celts and Italians. Most thought of themselves as Romans, members of a single empire. Within the walls, guarded by watchtowers, were tiled dwellings, taverns, and shady courtyards.

By 250 the Roman town was a center of trade. Merchants from the south sold wine and coral jewelry. They bought warm cloaks.

The shops of the forum surrounded the temple and law courts. The amphitheater was the scene of combat by gladiators. Beneath the curved roofs of the public baths, rich Romans soaked in the warm pools and gossiped.

Years of war

By the end of the fourth century, warriors were attacking the Roman empire on all fronts, and the legions soon withdrew from the province. Some Romans stayed on, together with those Celts who followed the Roman way of life. The town was soon under attack from all sides. Twice it was sacked and burned, and twice it was retaken. The public buildings lay in ruins. There was no money to rebuild them. Weeds grew in the cracked paving stones.

Word reached the town that the last Roman emperor had been overthrown by the Goths.

These were years of war and strife. Armies of pagan warriors swept across the land. Some remained and settled in the towns. They patched up the buildings and farmed the land as best they could. In 650 a Germanic–speaking army captured the town and founded a new kingdom.

Norman castle

By 800 the small kingdom had grown prosperous. Kings built churches and monasteries, where the monks cared for the sick and copied the scriptures.

Several times, fierce Viking pirates from Scandinavia sailed into the river mouth and attacked the town. Some of their descendants, known as Normans, were to conquer large areas of Europe, from England to Sicily.

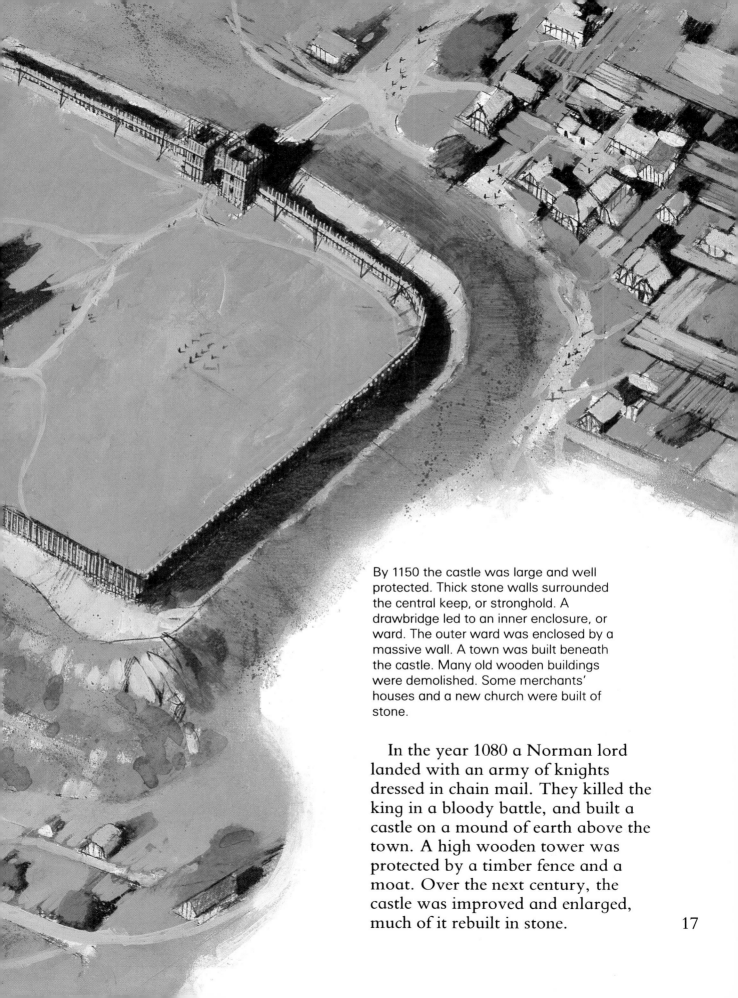

By 1150 the castle was large and well protected. Thick stone walls surrounded the central keep, or stronghold. A drawbridge led to an inner enclosure, or ward. The outer ward was enclosed by a massive wall. A town was built beneath the castle. Many old wooden buildings were demolished. Some merchants' houses and a new church were built of stone.

In the year 1080 a Norman lord landed with an army of knights dressed in chain mail. They killed the king in a bloody battle, and built a castle on a mound of earth above the town. A high wooden tower was protected by a timber fence and a moat. Over the next century, the castle was improved and enlarged, much of it rebuilt in stone.

17

Walled city

For the first time since the days of the Roman Empire, the city was large and prosperous. However, life had not been easy. The lord of the castle had rebelled against the king, and there had been long wars. The poor people had to work for the lord and pay high taxes. Much of their grain and meat was taken off in wagons to the castle. One year the peasants rioted and burned down the houses of the tax collectors. At another time there was a terrible outbreak of plague. The streets had no sewers and bred disease. Rats, ravens, and other animals scavenged among the rubbish.

In 1189, many of the townspeople left to fight the Crusades, wars in the Holy Land against the Muslims.

Most of the little ships in the river belonged to merchants trading in fish, wine, and wool.

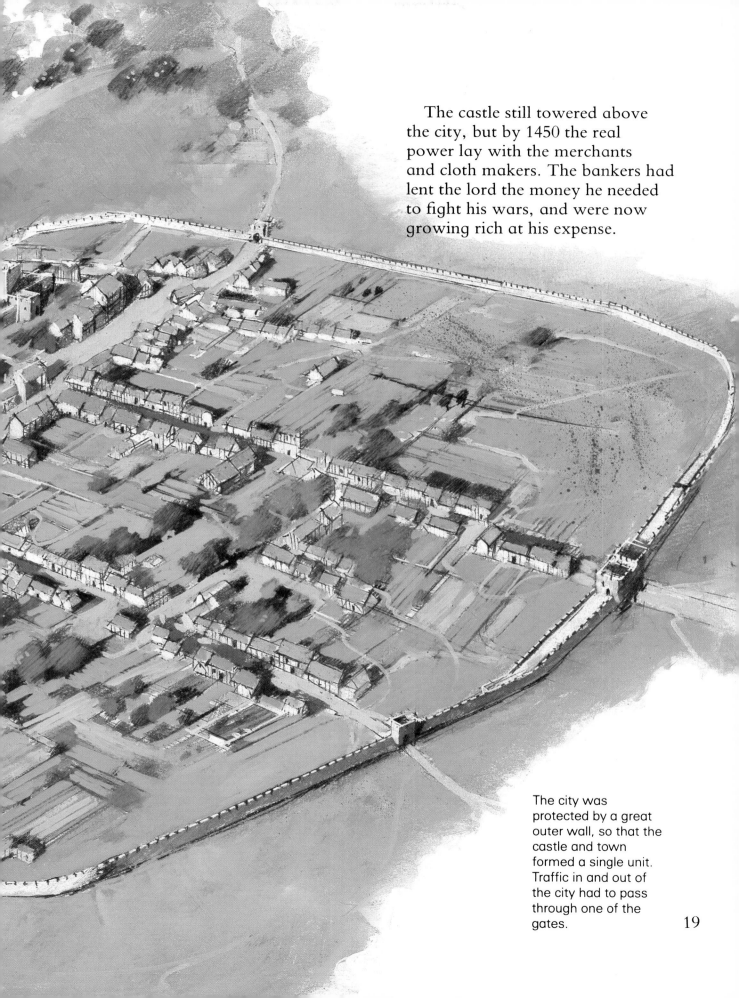

The castle still towered above the city, but by 1450 the real power lay with the merchants and cloth makers. The bankers had lent the lord the money he needed to fight his wars, and were now growing rich at his expense.

The city was protected by a great outer wall, so that the castle and town formed a single unit. Traffic in and out of the city had to pass through one of the gates.

Port for the New World

During the early 1500s the king became more and more powerful. The lord of the castle had to spend much of his time away at court, flattering the monarch. It did him little good, for in 1528 he had his head chopped off, accused of plotting to seize power. The castle soon became little more than a ruin.

Disagreements about religious beliefs resulted in two periods of wars. Even the thick city walls provided little defense against cannonballs and explosives.

Printing was now common, and people printed leaflets denouncing the power of the Pope, the leader of the Roman Catholic Church. The Protestants preached stern sermons.

The New World had been discovered by Christopher Columbus in 1492. Trade with the American colonies brought back strange new goods, such as tobacco. In 1620 a new harbor was built. The road to the city was lined with inns and the houses of rich ship owners.

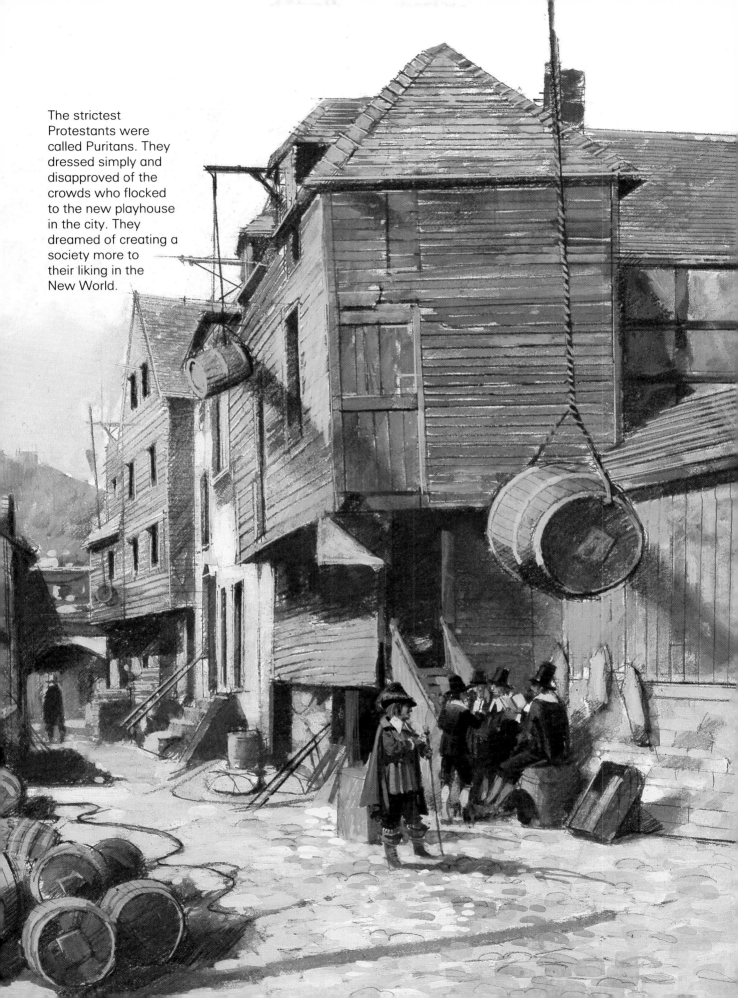

The strictest Protestants were called Puritans. They dressed simply and disapproved of the crowds who flocked to the new playhouse in the city. They dreamed of creating a society more to their liking in the New World.

The spreading city

In 1770 a traveler walking along the stony ridge would have seen a prosperous city stretching out below. It was still surrounded by open countryside and woodland. Stagecoaches carried visitors into the courtyard of a bustling inn. Carts brought in country produce for city markets.

The old castle lay in ruins, covered in ivy and overshadowed by leafy trees.

The city had always had its weavers, and had been exporting cloth since the time of the Romans. Now the wool of the sheep that still grazed the ridge was sent to a mill. Here the yarn was spun and then woven on new water-powered looms. A canal now skirted the city, linking the river mouth with large cities inland.

The old church still stood at the center of the city, surrounded by new buildings of brick or stone. The nobles lived outside the town in large country mansions, but they also owned elegant houses in the fashionable part of town. The finest houses belonged to merchants importing goods from the East Indies. 23

The age of industry

Never had the city seen so many changes. While much of Europe was still ruled by kings and queens, this city was now the chief port of a new republic, ruled by a president. The mad old king had been overthrown in the revolution of 1830.

Along the canal were new factories, their tall chimneys belching out black smoke. The workers' houses spread out along cobbled streets. Factory hours were long and wages were low. Men, women, and children struggled to earn a living. Many complained of

Factories were linked with the inland cities by a new railway, built in 1850. Coal, iron, steel, and food could now be transported faster.

These ships brought tea from China and cotton from India. They carried many people away forever to North America or Australia.

injustice and looked with envy toward the ridge, where the great houses of the factory owners were maintained by an army of servants and gardeners.

The city had swallowed up the countryside. The only trees to be seen were in parks and new churchyards.

Steam trains rattled over bridges. The masts of tall ships rose from the docks.

The age of science

From 1914 until 1918 the country was at war. Many young men marched away and never returned. Those who did return hoped to live in a new age, but many found only poverty and unemployment. This was, however, an age of science and technology. The gas works provided piped gas for each home. The power station generated electricity for light and industry.

Planes and sometimes airships could be seen soaring above the city, for an airfield had been built to the west. Steam trains and ships traveled farther and faster than ever before. Rich people went on ocean cruises to warmer lands. Others could not afford to travel abroad, but at least they could go to the movie theater and see silent films about faraway places.

By 1925 cars and motorcycles were a common sight on weekends, as people drove out to the countryside on fine new roads. They passed small houses and gardens, the homes of office workers who went to work in the city.

The smoke from factory chimneys still blackened the city's public buildings. The surrounding streets had changed little since the last century, and the wages for men and women were still low. In 1924 there had been a strike and rioting. Factory owners were worried. They had few orders for their goods, and the future looked uncertain.

The present

War returned to the city in 1940.
Enemy bombs rained down on the
factories, and many houses and shops
were also destroyed. Peace came in
1945, and by the 1960s new
buildings were rising.

"Good morning! This is your local radio traffic report. Vehicles are moving freely on the highway between exits 8 and 12. . ."

Viewed from the air, the city has changed. Great roads now snake their way between high-rise buildings.

There were tall office buildings and hotels built of concrete, steel, and glass. A modern soccer stadium was erected, and new parks were planted with trees.

New factories and apartment buildings were built in the suburbs. People enjoyed the modern comforts, but many missed the friendly atmosphere of their old neighborhoods. Children complained that there was nowhere to play. New hospitals and schools replaced the old buildings of the last century. A television antenna towered over the ridge. The old airfield was now the site of an international airport, linked to the city center by a six-lane superhighway and a subway.

29

The future

Earlier this year a new superhighway was built along the ridge. To everyone's surprise, a construction worker uncovered a Stone Age burial site. Flint axes and bone necklaces were unearthed and put in the Old Castle Museum. The guide told children the story of their city from the Stone Age. Then he guessed how the city might look in years ahead.

In the future, power might come from solar panels. No cars would pollute the air. Instead, people would be transported by robot-driven trains. Airbuses would take people to the suburbs. Many people would work at home on a computer network.

No one knows exactly what the city will look like in the future. But we can all see what a long and fascinating history the city has had.

Index